IN THE DOG KITCHEN

In the

Dog Kitchen

GREAT SNACK RECIPES FOR YOUR DOG

Julie Van Rosendaal

TouchWood Editions
touchwoodeditions.com

LIBRARY AND ARCHIVES CANADA CATALOGUING IN PUBLICATION
Van Rosendaal, Julie, 1970–, author
In the dog kitchen : great snack recipes for your dog /
Julie Van Rosendaal. — Revised and updated.

Includes index.
Issued in print and electronic formats.
ISBN 978-1-77151-105-6

1. Dogs—Food—Recipes. I. Title.

SF427.4.V35 2014   636.7'0855   C2014-901786-3

Editor: Cailey Cavallin
Proofreader: Christine Lyseng Savage
Design: Pete Kohut
Cover image: Quasarphoto, istockphoto.com
Food photography: Julie Van Rosendaal
Additional photo credits on p. 183

Canadian   Patrimoine
Heritage   canadien

We gratefully acknowledge the financial support for our publishing activities from the Canada Book Fund and the British Columbia Book Publishing Tax Credit.

This book was produced using FSC®-certified, acid-free papers, processed chlorine free, and printed with vegetable-based inks.

1 2 3 4 5 18 17 16 15 14

PRINTED IN CANADA

For Lou

Contents

Introduction

There are no beings on earth more capable of expressing unconditional love than dogs. When you want to return some of that adoration, there's no better delivery system than a homemade treat.

How we feed our pets is as affected by food trends as how we feed ourselves; in recent years, the quality of dog food—and treats—has increased to accommodate the demand for better ingredients, including organic ones. Gourmet dog biscuit companies—and even dog bakeries—have popped up, offering a variety of fancy treats. And the formulas have evolved to reflect our current tastes, incorporating ingredients like bison and quinoa and even going gluten free and grain free.

As we are becoming increasingly health conscious and focused on cooking at home, more pet owners are also willing to bake treats for their canine pals from scratch. Not only do homemade dog treats taste better than those that have been packed in cardboard and shipped around the world, they also allow you to have complete control over what goes into them. They also provide an opportunity to use up leftovers that might otherwise wind up in the garbage or compost bin, and you know they are free of additives, preservatives, and other ingredients you may not be able to pronounce. As a result they're good for the environment as well as for your dog. Most dog biscuit dough is simple and forgiving, and it can be baked in shapes and sizes to suit your dog, or packaged up to give as gifts that are always well received. (If you make your cookies smaller or larger than the average dog biscuit, adjust your baking time accordingly—or simply bake the cookies until they are firm or hard, as oven temperatures vary as well.)

When I wrote the first edition of this book, I was between dogs, but five years ago we adopted Lou, a big, happy black border collie/lab/husky cross, and our home hasn't been the same since. (Neither have our hardwood floors.) Now weighing around a hundred pounds, he loves a good treat as much as any dog, and so we got into the habit of experimenting with his favorite flavors—salmon, cheese, and peanut butter—in cookie form. Even though his idea of what makes a tasty treat differs greatly from ours, Lou loves

Lou

to be baked for as much as anyone. (Bonus: when they're dog treats, I don't wind up eating too many freshly baked goodies straight out of the oven myself.)

Lou's love for homemade cookies convinced me it was time to bring this old book back to life, with new recipes for the modern dog. I hope your pups enjoy them as much as Lou does!

What People Can Eat, But Dogs Can't

The recipes in this book use ingredients that are believed to be safe for dogs, although dogs' tastes (like people's) vary, and food allergies and intolerances are common in canines, just as they are in humans. Talk to your vet, and get to know what your dog likes (and dislikes) or might react negatively to. There are some ingredients, though, that can be harmful to all dogs, even if they are good for us. Here's what to avoid when making treats for your pup:

🦴 Chocolate is the number one craving among humans. Dogs love it too, but for them it can be deadly. It contains theobromine, which, when ingested by a dog in sufficient quantities, acts as a cardiac stimulant, releasing adrenaline that causes the heart to race or beat irregularly. Cocoa powder and baking chocolate are the most potent forms; dark chocolate contains nine times the theobromine of milk chocolate, and a few ounces can potentially kill a medium-size dog. Milk chocolate has the least amount of theobromine, so it is the least harmful. If you discover your dog has eaten chocolate, consult your vet immediately.

Carob chips and powder make excellent substitutes for chocolate in dog treats.

🦴 Coffee grounds or beans can cause symptoms similar to those of chocolate toxicity and can be just as serious.

🦴 Raisins, grapes, and related products such as juice and wine can also be harmful to canines. Many dogs love raisins, but these can cause kidney failure if consumed in large quantities.

🦴 Dogs lack the enzyme necessary to properly digest onions, so eating them can result in gas, vomiting, diarrhea, and general gastrointestinal distress.
NOTE: Garlic is in the onion family, but it is safe for your dog in small quantities, provided it is not raw. Fresh (baked into treats), dehydrated, and powdered garlic are safe for your dog in moderation. Some believe garlic acts as a flea repellant.

Gordon

Avocados have been reported to be harmful to dogs.

Macadamia nuts can cause gastrointestinal discomfort even if only a few are consumed.

Moldy or spoiled foods can cause food poisoning in animals as well as humans.

Xylitol, the zero-calorie sweetener, can be toxic and potentially fatal to dogs.

Rhubarb leaves are toxic if your dog ingests them.

Yeast dough will rise in the stomach if ingested, producing alcohol as it ferments. This will expand your dog's stomach uncomfortably and could lead to alcohol toxicity.

Louis

Making Dog Treats Grain Free

Going grain free, whether for reasons of health or by choice, can be tricky when it comes to baked goods; the same goes for dog treats. Fortunately, canine palates are more forgiving than ours—dogs appreciate a cookie made with chickpea flour or potato flakes far more than we likely would. I've added a completely new grain-free recipe section to this book (p. 85), but here are some tips for experimenting in your own kitchen.

There are plenty of dog-friendly ingredients—meats, cheese, veggies, fruit—that are already grain free and make tasty treats, but the trick is turning them into a dough that can be rolled, cut or shaped, and baked in cookie form. Fortunately, there are grain-free flours available that work well; most of the recipes in this book could be tweaked to be grain free by simply replacing the whole-wheat flour. Pop into your local health food store or peruse the bulk section of the grocery store (or even the baking aisle of larger grocery stores) and pick up a few alternative flours to experiment with, such as the ones listed on the next page.

🦴 Quinoa flour (quinoa is technically a seed, related to kale)

🦴 Buckwheat flour (buckwheat is also a seed, not a grain)

🦴 Chickpea or other legume flour (such as black bean or lentil)

🦴 Ground flaxseed (whole seeds can be ground at home in a spice mill)

🦴 Instant mashed potato flakes (make sure they're just potato—no seasonings)

Fortunately, dogs don't mind our mistakes, so you can go to town experimenting in the kitchen and coming up with your own grain-free combinations!

Miki

Most of the dog biscuits found in stores, from Milk-Bones to gourmet cookies, are rolled, cut into shapes, and baked until hard. Many of the recipes in this book can be turned into dough sturdy enough to roll and cut—just add a little more flour until the dough becomes malleable. Cut it into shapes and sizes suitable for your dog; avoid cutters with sharp or pointy edges (like stars). If you want to loop the cookies together with ribbon or twine for gift giving, poke a hole in each one with a straw before they go into the oven. Once they are baked, leaving your cookies in the oven for a couple of hours after turning it off will give them a chance to harden further.

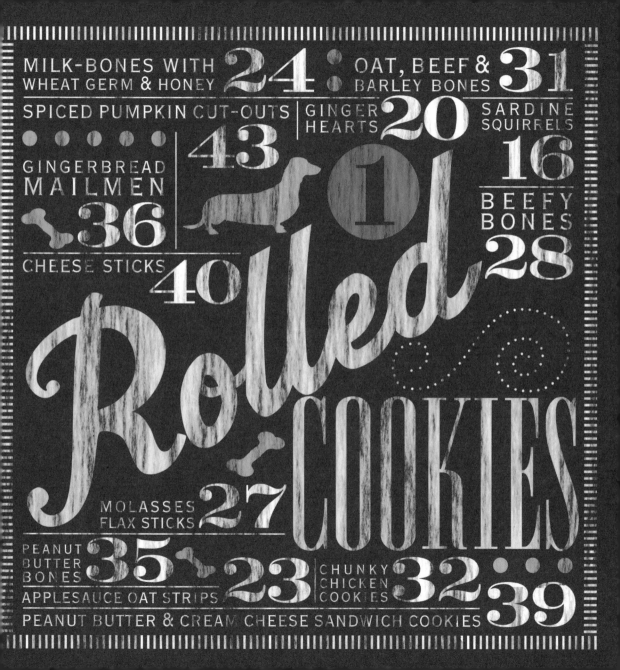

MILK-BONES WITH WHEAT GERM & HONEY **24**

OAT, BEEF & BARLEY BONES **31**

SPICED PUMPKIN CUT-OUTS

GINGER HEARTS **20**

SARDINE SQUIRRELS

43

1

16

GINGERBREAD MAILMEN

36

BEEFY BONES

28

CHEESE STICKS **40**

Rolled

COOKIES

MOLASSES FLAX STICKS **27**

PEANUT BUTTER BONES **35**

23

CHUNKY CHICKEN COOKIES **32**

39

APPLESAUCE OAT STRIPS

PEANUT BUTTER & CREAM CHEESE SANDWICH COOKIES

Sardine Squirrels

1 (3¾ oz) can sardines
   (packed in oil or water),
   undrained
½ cup chickpea flour
½ cup whole-wheat, oat,
   or barley flour
1 large egg

Doesn't the name alone make you want to bake a batch? This simple dough made with puréed sardines can be cut into any shapes you like—but if you can find a squirrel cookie cutter, all the better. Chickpea flour can be found at most health food stores. Or, if you prefer, substitute with more whole-wheat, oat, or barley flour.

Preheat the oven to 350°F. Line a baking sheet with parchment paper.

In the bowl of a food processor, pulse the sardines (with the liquid from the can), chickpea flour, whole-wheat flour, and egg until the dough comes together and forms a ball. (If the mixture is too wet and sticky, add more flour until the dough comes together.)

On a lightly floured surface, roll out the dough to about ¼-inch thick. Cut into whatever shapes you like. Place the cookies on the prepared baking sheet and bake for 20 to 30 minutes, until pale golden and firm. If you like, turn off the oven and leave the cookies inside to harden as they cool. Store in a tightly sealed container in the fridge, or freeze.

Ginger Hearts

Ginger Hearts

1 cup whole-wheat flour

1 cup old-fashioned or
    quick-cooking oats

1 cup oat bran

1 tsp powdered ginger
    (optional)

½ tsp cinnamon

½ cup plain yogurt

¼ cup milk or water

1 large egg

1 Tbsp grated fresh ginger
    (optional)

1 to 2 Tbsp honey
    or molasses

Cream cheese or peanut
    butter, for spreading
    (optional)

You can use either fresh or powdered ginger in these cookies—or both for extra-gingery treats. If you use powdered, add it along with the dry ingredients; if you use fresh, add it to the liquid mixture. If you don't have a heart-shaped cookie cutter, use the rim of a small glass, or cut the dough into easy shapes (like squares) with a sharp knife.

Preheat the oven to 350°F. Line 3 baking sheets with parchment paper.

In a large bowl, combine the flour, oats, oat bran, powdered ginger (if using), and cinnamon. In a small bowl, stir together the yogurt, milk, egg, fresh ginger (if using), and honey. Add the wet ingredients to the flour mixture and stir until well blended.

On a floured surface, knead the dough a few times, and then roll it out to about ¼-inch thick. Cut into hearts (or other shapes) with a cookie cutter or knife.

Transfer the cookies to the prepared baking sheets. If you like, poke a line of decorative holes along the edge of each cookie, about ¼ inch from the edge, with the tines of a fork or the end of a bamboo skewer.

Bake for 15 minutes, or until golden and firm. If you like, turn off the oven and leave the cookies inside to harden as they cool.

Once they have cooled completely, you can, if desired, spread the undersides of half the cookies with cream cheese and sandwich each of them with another cookie. Store in a tightly sealed container at room temperature if they're plain, or in the fridge if they're sandwiched with cream cheese.

Applesauce Oat Strips

MAKES ABOUT 3 DOZEN COOKIES

2 cups whole-wheat
   or barley flour
1 cup old-fashioned or
   quick-cooking oats
1 tsp cinnamon
½ cup applesauce
¼ cup water
1 large egg
1 Tbsp molasses or honey

These rolled cookies are like apple pie in bar form—they'll make your house smell wonderful as they bake. If you have juicy overripe pears around, grate one on a box grater and use it in place of the applesauce.

Preheat the oven to 350°F. Line 3 baking sheets with parchment paper.

In a large bowl, combine the flour, oats, and cinnamon. In a small bowl, stir together the applesauce, water, egg, and molasses. Add the applesauce mixture to the flour mixture and stir until well blended.

On a lightly floured surface, roll out the dough to about ¼-inch thick and cut into 1- x 3-inch strips (or other shapes) with a pastry cutter or knife.

Transfer the cookies to the prepared baking sheets and bake for about 20 minutes, until golden and firm. Let them cool on the sheets, or turn off the oven and leave the cookies inside to harden as they cool. Store in a tightly sealed container.

Charlie

Milk-Bones with Wheat Germ & Honey

2 cups whole-wheat flour

½ cup wheat germ

¼ cup skim milk powder

½ cup chicken stock
  or water

¼ cup canola oil

1 large egg

1 Tbsp honey or molasses

Here's a classic cookie that keeps well and dogs adore. A batch of homemade Milk-Bones wrapped in cellophane and tied with ribbon makes a great (and inexpensive!) gift for your favorite pooch. If you have a doughnut cutter, try cutting the treats into rings, then loop a ribbon through a whole stack.

Preheat the oven to 350°F. Line 3 baking sheets with parchment paper.

In a large bowl, combine the flour, wheat germ, and skim milk powder. In a small bowl, stir together the chicken stock, oil, egg, and honey. Add the wet ingredients to the dry ingredients and stir until well blended.

On a lightly floured surface, gently knead the dough a few times, and then roll it out to about ¼-inch thick. Cut into shapes with a cookie cutter or knife and transfer the cookies to the prepared baking sheets. Prick each cookie a few times with a fork.

Bake for about 20 minutes, until pale golden and firm. Turn off the oven and leave the cookies inside for a few hours to harden as they cool. Store in a tightly sealed container.

Molasses Flax Sticks

MAKES ABOUT 2 DOZEN COOKIES

2 cups whole-wheat flour

¼ cup ground flaxseed

½ tsp cinnamon

¼ cup canola oil

¼ cup dark molasses

¼ cup water

Harder biscuits keep better than those that have more moisture; let these cool and harden in the oven if you want your stash to last a long time.

Preheat the oven to 350°F. Line 2 baking sheets with parchment paper.

In a large bowl, combine the flour, flaxseed, and cinnamon. In a small bowl, stir together the oil, molasses, and water. Add to the flour mixture and stir until you have a soft dough.

On a lightly floured surface, roll out the dough to about ¼-inch thick. Cut into 1- x 3-inch strips (or other shapes) with a knife.

Transfer the cookies to the prepared baking sheets and bake for about 20 minutes, until firm. Let them cool on the sheets, or turn off the oven and leave the cookies inside for several hours to harden as they cool. Store in a tightly sealed container.

Beefy Bones

2 cups whole-wheat
   or barley flour
1 cup cornmeal
1 cup cooked and crumbled
   lean ground beef
¾ cup beef stock, tomato
   juice, or water
¼ cup canola oil
1 large egg

What's better than a beefy bone? If you're a dog—nothing.

Preheat the oven to 350°F. Line 3 baking sheets with parchment paper.

In a large bowl, combine the flour, cornmeal, and ground beef. In a small bowl, stir together the stock, oil, and egg. Add to the dry ingredients and mix until thoroughly blended.

On a lightly floured surface, roll out the dough to about ¼-inch thick and cut into shapes or 1- x 3-inch strips with a knife.

Place the cookies on the prepared baking sheets and bake for about 30 minutes, until firm. Turn off the oven and leave the cookies inside to harden as they cool. Store in a tightly sealed container in the fridge, or freeze.

Lemon

Oat, Beef & Barley Bones

MAKES ABOUT 1½ DOZEN COOKIES

½ cup old-fashioned or
quick-cooking oats
1 cup low-sodium
beef stock
1 large egg
1 cup barley, oat, or
whole-wheat flour

These treats are a great way to use up leftover oatmeal—just skip the stock and add a pinch of cinnamon. These would also taste great with an added handful of grated cheese.

Preheat the oven to 350°F. Line a baking sheet with parchment paper.

In a small saucepan, bring the oats and stock to a simmer; cook, stirring, until the oats are tender and look like oatmeal. Remove from heat and set aside to cool.

Once cooled, transfer the oats to a bowl and stir in the egg and flour. On a floured surface, roll out the dough to about ¼-inch thick and cut into bones or other shapes. Transfer the cookies to the prepared baking sheet and bake for 20 to 25 minutes, until pale golden on the bottom. The cookies will be a bit springy; if you want them to be firmer, bake them for an additional 5 to 10 minutes, and then turn off the oven and leave them inside to harden as they cool. Store in a tightly sealed container.

Chunky Chicken Cookies

8 oz ground chicken
   or turkey
1 cup oat or barley flour
1 cup whole-wheat flour
½ cup oat bran or
   wheat germ
½ cup chicken stock
   or water
1 large egg

Any ground meat would work well in these goodies—try squeezing sausage out of its casing and cooking it up for extra-tasty treats.

Preheat the oven to 350°F. Line 2 baking sheets with parchment paper.

In a heavy skillet over medium-high heat, cook the ground chicken, breaking it up with a spoon, until the meat is no longer pink.

In a large bowl, combine the oat flour, whole-wheat flour, and oat bran. In a small bowl or measuring cup, whisk together the stock (if you like, first pour it into the pan you cooked the chicken in to loosen any browned bits) and egg. Add to the dry ingredients along with the cooked chicken and stir until the dough comes together.

On a lightly floured surface, roll out the dough to ¼-inch thick and cut into rounds, rings, bones, or whatever shapes you like.

Place the cookies on the prepared baking sheets and bake for about 30 minutes, until firm. Turn off the oven and leave the cookies inside to harden as they cool. Store in a tightly sealed container in the fridge, or freeze.

Peanut Butter Bones

MAKES ABOUT 2 DOZEN BONES

2½ cups whole-wheat flour
½ cup old-fashioned or
   quick-cooking oats
½ cup chopped peanuts
   (optional)
1 cup peanut butter
1 cup water or milk
2 Tbsp honey

This is one of my most popular recipes. Most dogs go crazy for peanut butter. Use regular or chunky and make the bones as big or as small as you like—whatever suits your pooch.

Preheat the oven to 350°F. Line 2 baking sheets with parchment paper.

In a large bowl, combine the flour, oats, and peanuts (if using). Add the peanut butter, water, and honey, and stir until you have a stiff dough.

On a lightly floured surface, knead the dough until well blended, then roll it out to about ¼-inch thick. Cut into bones, shapes, or strips and place the cookies on the prepared baking sheets.

Bake for about 20 minutes, until golden. Let the cookies cool on the sheets, or turn off the oven and leave the cookies inside to harden as they cool. Store in a tightly sealed container.

Sally

Gingerbread Mailmen

2 cups whole-wheat flour
½ tsp cinnamon
½ tsp powdered ginger
¼ cup canola oil
¼ cup dark molasses
¼ cup water

These make a great gift, especially during the holidays. If you like, press in some carob chips or pieces of peanut for eyes before you bake the cookies.

Preheat the oven to 350°F. Line 2 baking sheets with parchment paper.

In a large bowl, combine the flour, cinnamon, and ginger. In a small bowl, stir together the oil, molasses, and water. Add to the dry ingredients and stir just until you have a soft dough.

On a lightly floured surface, roll out the dough to about ¼-inch thick. Cut into gingerbread men with a cookie cutter. (You can also make other shapes with a cookie cutter, the rim of a glass, or a knife.) Transfer the cookies to the prepared baking sheets.

Bake for 15 to 20 minutes, until firm. Let the cookies cool on the sheets, or turn off the oven and leave the cookies inside for several hours to harden as they cool. Store in a tightly sealed container.

Peanut Butter & Cream Cheese Sandwich Cookies

MAKES ABOUT 2½ DOZEN SANDWICHES

Cookies:
2 cups whole-wheat
  or barley flour
½ cup cornmeal
1 large egg
½ cup peanut butter
1½ cups water

Filling:
½ (8 oz) package cream
  cheese, at room
  temperature
¼ cup peanut butter
  (optional)
1 Tbsp honey (optional)

These cookies are completely adorable and perfect for gifting. If you're baking them for a friend, pack them in a Chinese takeout container lined with colorful tissue paper.

Preheat the oven to 350°F. Line 2 baking sheets with parchment paper.

In a large bowl, combine the flour, cornmeal, egg, peanut butter, and water, and stir until you have a soft dough. On a lightly floured surface, roll out the dough to about ¼-inch thick and cut into 1-inch rounds or other shapes with a cookie cutter or the rim of a small glass.

Place the cookies on the prepared baking sheets. Prick each cookie a few times with a fork—this will keep them from puffing up. Bake for about 15 minutes, until pale golden and firm. Let the cookies cool completely on the sheets.

To make the filling, beat the cream cheese with the peanut butter and honey (if using) until smooth. Spread half of the cooled cookies with the filling and top each with a second cookie. Store in a tightly sealed container in the fridge.

Tucker

Cheese Sticks

MAKES ABOUT 2 DOZEN COOKIES

2 cups whole-wheat
    or barley flour
½ cup old-fashioned or
    quick-cooking oats
½ cup grated cheddar
    cheese
¼ cup grated Parmesan
    cheese
1⅓ cups water
¼ cup canola oil
1 large egg

Cheese is universally adored by dogs. Here, it's baked into crunchy sticks you can carry around in your pocket.

Preheat the oven to 350°F. Line 2 baking sheets with parchment paper.

In a large bowl, combine the flour, oats, cheddar, and Parmesan. Add the water, oil, and egg, and stir or knead until you have a stiff dough.

On a lightly floured surface, roll out the dough to about ¼-inch thick. Cut into 1- x 2-inch sticks with a knife (or into other shapes with a cookie cutter). Place the cookies on the prepared baking sheets.

Bake for about 20 minutes, until golden and firm. If you like, turn off the oven and leave the cookies inside to harden as they cool. Store in a tightly sealed container.

Spiced Pumpkin Cut-Outs

MAKES ABOUT 2 DOZEN COOKIES

½ cup canned pure
   pumpkin
2 large eggs
¼ cup skim milk powder
2 cups whole-wheat, barley,
   or brown rice flour
½ tsp cinnamon

Cinnamon-spiked pumpkin cookies smell delicious in the oven during the holidays and are perfect for gift giving. Cut these cookies into whatever shapes and sizes are suitable for the occasion and the size of your dog.

Preheat the oven to 350°F. Line 2 baking sheets with parchment paper.

In a medium bowl, stir together the pumpkin, eggs, and skim milk powder. Add the flour and cinnamon, and stir until the dough comes together. Add more flour if the dough is too sticky to roll out.

On a lightly floured surface, roll out the dough to about ¼-inch thick. Cut into whatever shapes you like and place the cookies 1 inch apart on the prepared baking sheets.

Bake for 20 minutes, or until firm. If you like, turn off the oven and leave the cookies inside to harden as they cool. Store in a tightly sealed container.

Comox

Fancy shaped cookies are for having fun with—after all, our dogs can't appreciate our efforts in this regard, but it is still fun to make mini swirled cinnamon buns with cream cheese drizzle, crunchy pretzels, or puppy pizzas. Play around with your dog's favorite ingredients and make these treats your own. The recipes in this section are best suited to special occasions, or for giving as gifts.

PEANUT BUTTER & CARROT COOKIES 55

GRRRRANOLA STICKS 56

CINNAMON RICE WOOFLES 75 67

59 DOG SCOUT MINT COOKIES

PEANUT BUTTER OATMEAL ORBS

PEANUT BUTTER & SPINACH COOKIES

SQUASH COOKIES

76

2

64

PUPPY PANCAKES

SPICED HONEY CHEESE TWIRLS

63

52

47

TUNA SANDWICHES

Shaped

68

TRIPLE CHEESE BLISS

51 : COOKIES

COTTAGE CHEESE CORN DOGS

80

PUPPY PIZZAS

83

FISH BAIT

72

BANANA PEANUT BUTTER COOKIES

LENTIL CHEEZIES

48

60

79

CINNAMON BUN BITES

CRUNCHY CHICKEN PARMESAN PRETZELS

Spiced Honey Cheese Twirls

¾ cup cottage cheese
¼ cup canola or olive oil
2 Tbsp honey
1½ cups whole-wheat flour
1 tsp cinnamon
½ tsp baking powder

This soft dough can be shaped however you like. Kids might have fun making hearts, letters, and other special shapes for their pup.

Preheat the oven to 350°F. Line a baking sheet with parchment paper.

In a medium bowl, stir together the cottage cheese, oil, and honey. Add the flour, cinnamon, and baking powder, and stir until you have a soft dough.

Turn the dough out onto a floured surface and knead until well blended and smooth. Pinch off walnut-size pieces of dough and roll them into 2- to 3-inch ropes. Shape the dough ropes into rough circles, twirls, or other shapes, pinching the ends together to seal.

Place the cookies 1 inch apart on the prepared baking sheet and bake for 15 to 20 minutes, until golden. If you like, turn off the oven and leave the cookies inside to harden as they cool. Store in a tightly sealed container in the fridge, or freeze.

Cinnamon Bun Bites

MAKES ABOUT 2 DOZEN CINNAMON BUN BITES

2 cups whole-wheat flour

1 tsp baking powder

Pinch salt

½ cup water or milk

¼ cup canola oil

1 large egg

1 to 2 Tbsp honey

½ tsp cinnamon

2 to 3 Tbsp cream cheese, at room temperature, for drizzling (optional)

These are one of my favorite treats. They look like teeny cinnamon buns! To complete the effect, drizzle them with cream cheese that has been thinned with a little honey or water.

Preheat the oven to 350°F. Line 2 baking sheets with parchment paper.

In a large bowl, combine the flour, baking powder, and salt. In a small bowl, stir together the water, oil, and egg. Add to the dry ingredients and stir just until you have a soft dough.

On a lightly floured surface, roll out the dough into an 8- x 14-inch rectangle. Drizzle with the honey and sprinkle with the cinnamon. Starting from a long edge, roll the dough up jelly-roll style. Pinch along the edge to seal the roll. Using a sharp, serrated knife or dental floss, slice the roll into slices, ¼-inch to ½-inch thick. Place the slices on the prepared baking sheets.

Bake for about 15 minutes, until springy to the touch. Remove from the oven and allow to cool.

Thin the cream cheese, if using, by stirring or beating it with about 1 tablespoon of water. Place the mixture in a ziplock bag, snip off a corner of the bag, and drizzle the cream cheese over the cooled treats. Store in a tightly sealed container for a couple of days, or freeze for longer storage.

Cottage Cheese Corn Dogs

MAKES ABOUT 2 DOZEN MINI CORN DOGS

2 cups whole-wheat
  or barley flour
1 cup cornmeal
1 tsp baking powder
1 cup cottage cheese
1 cup chicken stock
  or buttermilk
1 large egg
2 to 3 uncooked hot dogs
  or cooked breakfast
  sausages, cut into
  ½-inch pieces

These wee corn dogs are made with chunks of real hot dog (universally adored by dogs) baked into cornmeal batter in mini muffin pans. No need for the sticks.

Preheat the oven to 350°F.

In a large bowl, combine the flour, cornmeal, and baking powder. In a small bowl, stir together the cottage cheese, stock, and egg. Add to the dry ingredients and stir just until blended.

Coat mini muffin pans with nonstick spray and fill each cup halfway with batter. Press a piece of hot dog into each cup. Bake for about 20 minutes, until the corn dogs are golden and springy to the touch. Remove from the pan with a thin knife and transfer to a wire rack to cool. Store in a tightly sealed container in the fridge, or freeze.

Schutt

Tuna Sandwiches

1 (6 oz) can tuna, salmon, or sardines (packed in water), undrained
½ cup water
¼ cup canola or olive oil
2 cups whole-wheat or barley flour
1 cup cornmeal
1 (8 oz) tub spreadable cream cheese, at room temperature (optional)

These fishy cookies are delicious regardless of whether you use the cream cheese filling. Oily fish are rich in vitamin D, which aids in the absorption of calcium and contributes to healthy bones and teeth.

Preheat the oven to 350°F. Line 2 baking sheets with parchment paper.

In the bowl of a food processor, combine the tuna (with the liquid from the can), water, and oil. Pulse until well blended and relatively smooth. In a large bowl, combine the flour and cornmeal. Add the tuna mixture to the flour mixture and stir until you have a soft dough.

Roll the dough into walnut-size balls and place them on the prepared baking sheets. Press each dough ball down once or twice (crisscrossed) with the back of a fork, like you would a peanut butter cookie.

Bake for about 15 minutes, until pale golden and firm. Let the cookies cool completely on the sheets or on a wire rack. If you like, spread the bottoms of half the cookies with cream cheese and sandwich each with another cookie. Store in a tightly sealed container in the fridge.

Peanut Butter & Carrot Cookies

MAKES ABOUT 2 DOZEN COOKIES

2 cups whole-wheat
   or barley flour
½ cup peanut butter
¾ cup carrot juice
1 large egg

It's no secret that dogs love peanut butter, which goes surprisingly well with carrots. You can buy pure carrot juice at health food stores, or make your own if you happen to have a juicer.

Preheat the oven to 350°F. Line 2 baking sheets with parchment paper.

In a large bowl, stir together the flour, peanut butter, carrot juice, and egg, mixing until you have a soft dough.

Roll the dough into 1-inch balls and place them a couple of inches apart on the prepared baking sheets. Flatten each cookie with the back of a fork.

Bake for about 15 minutes, until firm. Let the cookies cool on the sheets, or turn off the oven and leave the cookies inside to harden as they cool. Store in a tightly sealed container.

Grrrranola Sticks

2 cups whole-wheat flour

1 cup old-fashioned oats or
rolled barley flakes

½ cup oat bran or
wheat germ

½ cup cornmeal

½ cup finely chopped
walnuts

¼ cup pumpkin, sunflower,
or sesame seeds

¼ cup skim milk powder
(optional)

1½ cups chicken stock,
milk, or water

1 large egg

Beaten egg or milk, for
brushing (optional)

Whole grains, nuts, and seeds deliver fiber, protein, healthy fats, and a host of essential vitamins and minerals. Feel free to experiment with different varieties of each.

Preheat the oven to 325°F. Line 3 baking sheets with parchment paper.

In a large bowl, combine the flour, oats, oat bran, cornmeal, walnuts, seeds, and skim milk powder (if using). In a small bowl, whisk together the stock and egg. Add to the dry ingredients and stir until well blended. The dough should be a bit sticky; let it sit in the bowl for 30 minutes to allow the grains to absorb some of the excess moisture. If it's still too sticky, add a little more flour.

Roll the dough into ropes, then cut into sections, or roll out on a floured surface to about ¼-inch thick and cut into shapes or sticks. Place the cookies on the prepared baking sheets, and, if you like, brush the tops with a little beaten egg.

Bake for about 40 minutes, then turn off the oven and leave the cookies inside to harden as they cool. Store in a tightly sealed container.

Dog Scout Mint Cookies

MAKES ABOUT 2 DOZEN COOKIES

2 cups whole-wheat
or barley flour
½ cup wheat germ, plus
extra for rolling
¼ cup skim milk powder
¼ cup dried mint
1 cup water
2 Tbsp canola oil

If your little buddy is going to have dog breath, it might as well be minty.

Preheat the oven to 350°F. Line 2 baking sheets with parchment paper.

In a large bowl, combine the flour, wheat germ, skim milk powder, and mint. Add the water and oil, and stir until you have a soft dough.

Roll the dough into 1-inch balls, then roll the balls in wheat germ to coat. Place on the prepared baking sheets and flatten each cookie with the back of a fork.

Bake for about 20 minutes, until firm. If you like, turn off the oven and leave the cookies inside to harden as they cool. Store in a tightly sealed container.

Walter

Crunchy Chicken Parmesan Pretzels

MAKES ABOUT 2 DOZEN PRETZELS

2½ cups whole-wheat flour

¼ cup skim milk powder

¼ cup grated Parmesan cheese

1 cup chicken stock or water

2 Tbsp canola oil

1 egg, beaten, for brushing (optional)

Grated Parmesan cheese or sesame seeds, for sprinkling (optional)

Stocks are great to use in dog cookies because they add flavor and protein. But try to use real stock instead of canned stock or bouillon cubes, which contain high quantities of salt and additives such as MSG. (To make your own, place a chicken carcass in a pot, cover with water, bring to a boil, and simmer for an hour, then allow to cool and strain.)

Preheat the oven to 375°F. Line 2 baking sheets with parchment paper.

In a large bowl, combine the flour, skim milk powder, and Parmesan. Add the stock and oil, and stir until you have a stiff dough.

Pinch off 1-inch pieces of dough, roll them into thin ropes, and shape the ropes into pretzels, pressing the ends to seal. (You can make the pretzels bigger or smaller to suit the size of your dog, but be sure to increase or decrease the baking time accordingly.) If you like, brush a little beaten egg over the tops of the pretzels and sprinkle with extra Parmesan or sesame seeds.

Place the pretzels on the prepared baking sheets and bake for about 20 minutes, until firm. Turn off the oven and leave the pretzels inside to harden as they cool. Store in a tightly sealed container.

Peanut Butter Oatmeal Orbs

MAKES ABOUT 5 DOZEN TREATS

1 cup whole-wheat
   or oat flour
2 cups old-fashioned or
   quick-cooking oats
1 tsp baking soda
¾ cup peanut butter
¾ cup water or carrot juice
2 Tbsp honey
1 large egg
½ cup chopped peanuts
¼ cup sunflower and/or
   pumpkin seeds

These bite-size snacks make perfect training treats; keep a ziplock bag of them in your pocket when you take your dog for a walk.

Preheat the oven to 350°F. Line 3 or 4 baking sheets with parchment paper.

In a large bowl, stir together the flour, oats, and baking soda. Add the peanut butter, water, honey, and egg, and mix until well blended. Stir in the peanuts and seeds.

Roll the dough into small balls the size of marbles (or larger balls, according to the size of your dog) and place on the prepared baking sheets. If you like, press down on each ball with a fork or make an X using a bamboo skewer. Bake for 10 to 15 minutes, until golden and firm. Store in a tightly sealed container.

Puppy Pancakes

1 cup whole-wheat
   or barley flour
1 tsp baking powder
1 cup water or milk
2 Tbsp bacon or chicken
   drippings or canola oil
1 large egg
½ cup blueberries, grated
   cheese, or mashed
   banana (optional)

These teeny pancakes are adorable, and perfect for puppies and older dogs who have difficulty with hard biscuits. If you like, stir ½ cup fresh blueberries, mashed banana, or grated cheese into the batter. If you cook the pancakes in a pan that you've just cooked ground beef or bacon in, it will infuse the pancakes with the flavor of the meat.

In a large bowl, stir together the flour and baking powder. Then, in a small bowl, stir together the water, drippings, and egg; add to the flour mixture and stir just until combined. If you like, gently stir in the blueberries or other optional ingredient.

Coat a large skillet with nonstick spray and place over medium heat. Cook a couple of tablespoons of batter at a time, making silver-dollar-size pancakes, until bubbles rise to the surface of the pancakes and the bottoms are golden brown, about 2 to 4 minutes. Flip the pancakes and cook for another minute or two. Repeat with the remaining batter. Let the pancakes cool completely before serving. Store in a tightly sealed container in the fridge, or freeze.

Peanut Butter & Spinach Cookies

1 cup packed baby spinach

1 cup water

2 cups whole-wheat or barley flour

1/2 cup peanut butter

1 large egg

Peanut butter and spinach are a winning combination—in curries (for people) and cookies (for dogs). These cookies are a great way to use up the last of your greens when they start to wilt.

Preheat the oven to 350°F. Line 2 baking sheets with parchment paper.

In a blender or food processor, pulse the spinach and water until the mixture is as smooth as you can get it.

In a large bowl, stir together the flour, peanut butter, egg, and spinach mixture, blending until you have a soft dough. (Alternatively, if using a food processor, add the flour, peanut butter, and egg to the bowl of the food processor once the spinach mixture is smooth and pulse until the dough forms a ball. Note: This won't work in a blender.)

Roll the dough into 1-inch balls and place them a couple of inches apart on the prepared baking sheets. Flatten each cookie with the back of a fork.

Bake for about 15 minutes, until firm. Let the cookies cool on the sheets, or turn off the oven and leave the cookies inside to harden as they cool. Store in a tightly sealed container.

Riley

Triple Cheese Bliss

MAKES ABOUT 2 DOZEN COOKIES

½ cup cottage cheese
½ cup grated cheddar cheese
½ cup grated Parmesan cheese
2 Tbsp canola oil
2 Tbsp water
1 large egg
2 cups whole-wheat flour

This is what dogs dream about at night—three cheeses, baked into a crunchy cookie.

Preheat the oven to 350°F. Line 2 baking sheets with parchment paper.

In the bowl of a food processor, combine the cottage cheese, cheddar, and Parmesan, along with the oil, water, and egg, and pulse until well blended. Add the flour and pulse until the dough comes together. It may look crumbly, but it will be sticky and easy to shape.

Roll the dough into 1-inch balls and place them 1 inch apart on the prepared baking sheets. Press down on each ball once or twice with the back of a fork, like you would a peanut butter cookie.

Bake for 15 to 20 minutes, until golden and firm. Let the cookies cool on the sheets, or turn off the oven and leave them inside to harden as they cool. Store in a tightly sealed container, or freeze.

**Mackie (left) and
Tonka (right)**

Fish Bait

Fish Bait

1 (6 oz) can salmon, tuna, or sardines (packed in oil or water), undrained
¼ cup canola or olive oil
3 cups whole-wheat flour
1 cup cornmeal

Most dogs adore the flavor of fish—so much so that you may be able to use these treats as bait for your dog. Oily fish varieties like salmon and sardines deliver a dose of omega-3 fatty acids, which contribute to a healthy coat. There are many ways to prepare these cookies, including the two outlined below. You can also roll the dough out on a floured surface and cut it into shapes, or treat it like biscotti: pat the dough into a log and bake it, then cut the log into slices and bake the slices until firm and dry. Adjust the size of the cookies to suit your pup.

Preheat the oven to 350°F. Coat a baking sheet with nonstick spray.

Put the salmon (with the liquid from the can) into the bowl of a food processor, then fill the can with water and add that too. Add the oil and process until smooth. (Alternatively, mash the mixture really well with a potato masher or fork.)

In a large bowl, stir together the flour and cornmeal. Add the salmon mixture and stir until you have a soft, sticky dough.

Roll out the dough to about ¼-inch thick on the prepared baking sheet. Cut the dough lengthwise into strips, then crosswise into sticks of whatever length you like. If you want the treats to be firm, pull apart the sticks so that they bake from all sides; otherwise, leave them as is, and you'll easily be able to break them into sticks once baked.

Alternatively, roll the dough into walnut-size balls and place them on parchment-lined baking sheets. Press down on each ball once or twice with the back of a fork, like you would a peanut butter cookie.

Bake for 25 to 30 minutes, until firm. Let the cookies cool on the sheet, or turn off the oven and leave the cookies inside to harden as they cool. Store in a tightly sealed container. If they still contain some moisture, keep in the fridge.

Cinnamon Rice Woofles

MAKES ABOUT 8 LARGE WAFFLES, EACH OF WHICH SHOULD DIVIDE INTO 4 SMALLER WAFFLES

3 cups whole-wheat flour

2 tsp baking powder

1 tsp cinnamon

1 cup cooked brown
rice or barley

2 large eggs

2 Tbsp canola oil

2 cups milk, water,
or chicken stock

These crispy treats are made in your waffle iron. They make great use of leftover cooked grains and are perfect for larger dog breeds.

In a large bowl, combine the flour, baking powder, and cinnamon. Add the rice, eggs, oil, and milk, and stir just until blended.

Preheat your waffle iron and coat it with nonstick spray. Pour about ⅓ cup of the batter onto the iron (or use a quantity suitable for your iron), spreading it out. Close the lid and cook until the waffle is golden and crisp. Repeat with the rest of the batter. Store in a tightly sealed container, or freeze.

Squash Cookies

MAKES ABOUT 1½ DOZEN COOKIES

2 cups whole-wheat flour
¼ cup ground flaxseed
½ tsp baking soda
½ tsp cinnamon
1 cup mashed or puréed
  cooked winter squash, or
  canned pure pumpkin
¼ cup canola or olive oil
2 Tbsp molasses or honey

Nutrient-dense winter squash (think acorn, butternut, or hubbard) is as good for dogs as it is for people, delivering plenty of fiber and beta-carotene with very few calories. Its natural sweetness is appealing to pups, and combined with cinnamon, it smells like pumpkin pie baking in the oven.

Preheat the oven to 350°F. Line a baking sheet with parchment paper.

In a large bowl, combine the flour, flaxseed, baking soda, and cinnamon. In a small bowl, stir together the squash, oil, and molasses. Add to the flour mixture and stir until you have a soft dough.

Roll the dough into 1-inch balls (or make them a size appropriate for your dog) and place them 1 or 2 inches apart on the prepared baking sheet. Press down on each cookie once or twice with a fork, like you would a peanut butter cookie.

Bake for 15 to 20 minutes, or until firm. Let the cookies cool on the sheet, or turn off the oven and leave the cookies inside to harden as they cool. Store in a tightly sealed container for 2 to 3 days; refrigerate or freeze if the cookies contain chunks of squash.

Banana Peanut Butter Cookies

½ cup peanut butter
2 ripe bananas, mashed
1 large egg
2 Tbsp honey
¾ cup water
2 cups whole-wheat flour
1 tsp baking powder

These soft, cakey cookies are perfect for older dogs that have difficulty chewing harder biscuits.

Preheat the oven to 350°F. Line 2 baking sheets with parchment paper.

In a large bowl, combine the peanut butter, bananas, egg, honey, and water. Add the flour and baking powder and stir until well combined.

Drop the dough by the spoonful onto the prepared baking sheets. Bake for about 15 minutes, until springy to the touch. Store in a tightly sealed container in the fridge, or freeze.

Monty

Lentil Cheezies

MAKES ABOUT 3 DOZEN COOKIES

½ cup dry red lentils

2 cups grated old cheddar cheese

1 cup old-fashioned or quick-cooking oats

1 Tbsp ground flaxseed

Once baked, these treats will be puffy and crunchy. But the uncooked dough will have the texture of mashed potatoes; feel free to squish the cookies with a spoon before sliding them into the oven. For a variation, add flour to make a stiff dough that can be rolled and cut into shapes.

Preheat the oven to 400°F. Line 3 baking sheets with parchment paper.

Place the lentils in a small saucepan and cover with water; bring to a boil and simmer for 12 to 14 minutes, until very tender. Drain and transfer to the bowl of a food processor.

Add the cheddar, oats, and flaxseed to the lentils and pulse until well blended, scraping down the sides of the bowl once or twice.

Drop the mixture by the spoonful onto the prepared baking sheets. Bake for 20 minutes, until pale golden and set. Let the cookies cool completely on the sheets. Store in a tightly sealed container in the fridge.

Puppy Pizzas

MAKES ABOUT 3 DOZEN MINI PIZZAS

2 cups whole-wheat
   or barley flour
½ cup water
¼ cup olive or canola oil
1 large egg
¼ cup tomato paste
½ tsp dried parsley
   or oregano
¼ cup freshly grated
   Parmesan cheese

How cute are teeny pizzas for your dog? They can be topped with cooked ground beef or bits of ham as well.

Preheat the oven to 350°F. Line 3 baking sheets with parchment paper.

Put the flour in a large bowl. In a small bowl, whisk together the water, oil, and egg; add to the flour and stir until you have a soft dough. Add a little extra flour if the dough is too sticky.

On a lightly floured surface, roll out the dough to about ¼-inch thick. Cut into small rounds with a cookie cutter, the rim of a glass, or the open end of the tomato paste can, and transfer to the prepared baking sheets.

Spread the dough rounds with the tomato paste and sprinkle with the parsley and Parmesan.

Bake for about 15 minutes, until slightly puffed and pale golden around the edges. Store in a tightly sealed container in the fridge, or freeze.

Tucker

Shaped Cookies / 83

Grain-free eating has been all the rage recently. Whether your pup is on a grain-free diet for reasons of health or by choice (yours!), here are some delicious ways to satisfy his or her cookie cravings without a grain in sight. Quinoa and buckwheat are technically seeds, not grains; in flour form they're perfect for making sturdy grain-free dough. Other treats in this section are made with chickpea flour or instant mashed potato flakes, and some are purely meat—but all will have your dog begging for more.

Grain-Free Treats

PEANUT BUTTER, BANANA & BACON BROWNIES

GRILLED CHEESE & TOMATO SOUP BITES 94

93 PEANUT BUTTER FLAX COOKIES

102

CHICKEN & SPINACH QUINOA COOKIES

CINNAMON BANANA THUMBPRINTS

CHICKEN & TUNA LEATHER 89 126

OVEN-DRIED CHICKEN JERKY

113

90 SARDINE & FLAXSEED BITES

86

TV DINNER TREATS

125 TUNA TATER TOTS

122

MEAT & POTATO TREATS 105

101

CHICKEN & BACON TREATS

TREATS

HAM & BUCKWHEAT COOKIES 98

129

CHEESY SWEET POTATO TREATS

BEEF & BUCKWHEAT BONES 118

PEANUT BUTTER & BANANA TREATS

114

TUNA, CHICKPEA & POTATO COOKIES

97 106

BUBBLE & SQUEAK BITES

FISHY CHICKPEA TREATS

BABY FOOD BITES

GINGER & CINNAMON SWEET POTATO FLAX SQUIGGLES 110

117

121

Oven-Dried Chicken Jerky

Skinless, boneless chicken breasts, trimmed of any fat

We buy containers of dried chicken strips on Vancouver Island every summer for Lou. He adores them, and it turns out they're fairly simple to make. All you need are some chicken breasts—they work better than thighs, which are difficult to slice thinly and contain more fat (which doesn't dry out completely).

Preheat the oven to 200°F. Line a baking sheet with parchment paper, or spray it with nonstick spray.

On a cutting board, pat the chicken breasts dry with paper towels. Slice as thin as you can and place on the prepared baking sheet, leaving about half an inch between each piece.

Bake for 3 hours, until completely dry and leathery. Let the jerky cool completely, and then store in an airtight container. (Note: These must be completely dried out in order to store well. If they aren't, keep them in the fridge or freezer.)

Chicken & Tuna Leather

MAKES ABOUT 3 DOZEN TREATS

1 skinless, boneless chicken breast, trimmed of fat

1 (6 oz) can tuna (packed in water), undrained

Everyone knows fruit leather. This is the same thing, only made with meat. Simply purée chicken with a can of tuna, and then spread the mixture out thin on a baking sheet and dry it out in the oven. Cut into bits or strips and voilà— all-meat treats.

Preheat the oven to 300°F. Line a baking sheet with parchment paper.

Cut the chicken into chunks. In the bowl of a food processor, purée the chicken and tuna (with the liquid from the can) until you have a smooth paste.

Scrape out onto the prepared baking sheet. Spread the mixture out so that it's about ¼-inch thick and as even as you can get it. Bake for 1 hour, or until golden and leathery.

Cut into pieces with scissors or a sharp knife. Store extras in a container in the fridge.

Lou

Sardine & Flaxseed Bites

1 (3¾ oz) can sardines
(packed in oil or water),
undrained

1 large egg

⅓ to ½ cup ground flaxseed

These fishy treats won't make your house smell fantastic as they bake, but your dog will adore them.

Preheat the oven to 350°F. Line a baking sheet with parchment paper.

In the bowl of a food processor, pulse the sardines (with the liquid from the can), egg, and flaxseed until well blended and relatively smooth.

Drop the dough by the small spoonful onto the prepared baking sheet, and press down on each cookie with the back of a spoon. (If it sticks, dip the spoon in water.)

Bake for 15 to 20 minutes, until firm. If you like, turn off the oven and leave the cookies inside to harden as they cool. Store in a tightly sealed container in the fridge, or freeze.

Peanut Butter Flax Cookies

MAKES ABOUT 1½ DOZEN COOKIES

½ cup chunky
   peanut butter
1 large egg
½ cup ground flaxseed

These nutty, peanut buttery treats are high in fiber and omega-3 fatty acids—and they're one of Lou's favorites. If you like, swap the flaxseed for large-flake oats, pulsed into a coarse flour.

Preheat the oven to 350°F.

In a medium bowl, stir together the peanut butter, egg, and flaxseed until well blended and smooth.

Roll the mixture into marble-size balls and place them on an ungreased baking sheet. Press down on each cookie with a fork to flatten, like you would a peanut butter cookie.

Bake for 15 to 20 minutes, until golden and firm. If you like, turn off the oven and leave the cookies inside to harden as they cool.

Grilled Cheese & Tomato Soup Bites

½ (10 oz) can condensed
    tomato soup
1 cup grated cheddar cheese
⅔ cup instant mashed
    potato flakes

Okay, these aren't actually grilled—but the name was irresistible. Tomato soup, grated cheddar, and potato flakes make simple, tasty treats that are soft and delicious.

Preheat the oven to 350°F. Line 2 baking sheets with parchment paper.

In the bowl of a food processor, pulse the tomato soup, cheddar, and potato flakes until well blended and relatively smooth. Let sit for 5 to 10 minutes to allow the mixture to firm up as the potato flakes absorb the liquid. Then roll out the dough about ½-inch thick and cut into rounds, squares, or shapes (they will puff up and lose their shape slightly). Place the treats on the prepared baking sheets.

Bake for 15 minutes, or until puffed and set. The treats will be dark golden on the bottom. Let them cool on the sheets, and then peel them off the parchment paper. Store in a tightly sealed container in the fridge, or freeze.

Tuna, Chickpea & Potato Cookies

MAKES ABOUT 2 DOZEN COOKIES

1 (6 oz) can tuna or salmon
(packed in oil or water),
undrained
1 cup instant mashed
potato flakes
1 (19 oz) can chickpeas,
drained
2 large eggs

Canned chickpeas add fiber-rich, nutrient-dense structure to these cookies, which are further bulked up with potato flakes. Canned tuna or salmon makes these goodies irresistible.

Preheat the oven to 350°F. Line 2 baking sheets with parchment paper.

In the bowl of a food processor, pulse the tuna (with the liquid from the can) and potato flakes until well blended. Scrape down the sides of the bowl and let the mixture sit for a few minutes—this will allow the potato flakes to absorb some of the moisture from the tuna. Add the chickpeas and eggs and pulse until you have a smooth dough that can be shaped into a ball. If the dough is too moist, add more potato flakes.

Roll the mixture into 1-inch balls and place the balls a couple of inches apart on the prepared baking sheets. Press down on each cookie with a fork (dip it in water to keep it from sticking). Bake for 15 to 20 minutes, until golden and set. Store in a tightly sealed container in the fridge, or freeze.

Ham & Buckwheat Cookies

MAKES ABOUT 2 DOZEN COOKIES

1 cup chopped cooked ham

½ cup water or
   chicken stock

1 large egg

1 cup buckwheat, quinoa,
   or chickpea flour

Smoky, flavorful roast ham makes for a tasty (dog) cookie—
and if you've baked a ham, you likely have leftovers to work
with. These treats work well with buckwheat or quinoa flour
(both are seeds, not grains), chickpea flour, or even instant
mashed potato flakes.

Preheat the oven to 350°F. Grease 2 baking sheets, or line
them with parchment paper.

   In the bowl of a food processor, pulse the ham, water, and
egg until the mixture is as well blended and smooth as you can
get it. Don't worry about small chunks.

   Add the flour and pulse until you have a soft dough. Roll
into 1-inch balls and place them 1 inch apart on the prepared
baking sheets. For smaller cookies, roll the dough into smaller
balls. Press down on each cookie with a fork (dip it in water to
keep it from sticking).

   Bake for 20 minutes, until firm. If you like, turn off the
oven and leave the cookies inside to harden as they cool. Store
in a tightly sealed container in the fridge, or freeze.

Chicken & Bacon Treats

MAKES ABOUT 50 TREATS

1 large skinless, boneless
   chicken breast, cubed
2 to 3 Tbsp bacon drippings
1 large egg

These all-meat treats are made with puréed chicken, spread into a pan and baked. If you like, spread the batter even thinner on a baking sheet and bake at a low temperature for a couple of hours, until dry and leathery. Cut into pieces or strips with scissors.

Preheat the oven to 350°F. Line an 8- x 8-inch pan with parchment paper.

In the bowl of a food processor, pulse the chicken, bacon drippings, and egg until perfectly smooth, scraping down the sides of the bowl.

Scrape into the prepared pan and spread out to an even thickness. Bake for 20 minutes, or until cooked through and springy to the touch.

Allow to cool, and then cut into small squares appropriate for the size of your dog. Store in a tightly sealed container in the fridge, or freeze.

Peanut Butter, Banana & Bacon Brownies

MAKES ABOUT 1 DOZEN BROWNIES

4 slices bacon, chopped

1 large ripe banana

¼ cup peanut butter

½ (19 oz) can chickpeas, drained (1 cup)

1 large egg

If you're after something more birthday party-ish, reserve the bacon pieces, then spread the cooled bars with softened cream cheese thinned with a little water or milk and sprinkle the bacon pieces overtop.

Preheat the oven to 350°F. Grease an 8- x 8-inch or 9- x 9-inch pan, or line with parchment paper.

In a small skillet over medium-high heat, cook the bacon until crisp. Set aside. Pour off the drippings and reserve.

In the bowl of a food processor, pulse the banana, peanut butter, chickpeas, egg, and bacon drippings until smooth—it will look like hummus. Pour the batter into the prepared pan and sprinkle the cooked bacon pieces overtop.

Bake for 30 minutes, until springy to the touch.

Allow to cool completely in the pan before cutting into squares or bars. Store in a tightly sealed container in the fridge, or freeze.

Meat & Potato Treats

MAKES ABOUT 1½ DOZEN TREATS

1 cup canned meaty dog food
(not chunks in gravy)
1 cup instant mashed
potato flakes
1 large egg
⅓ cup water

Whether or not you feed your dog canned food, it works well as a base for treats. Go for the classic soft and meaty dog food, rather than chunks in gravy. (And if you're going grain free, read the ingredient list to ensure it doesn't contain any.) Potato flakes and egg provide the stability to turn dog food into treats.

Preheat the oven to 400°F. Line a baking sheet with parchment paper.

In a medium bowl, stir together the dog food, potato flakes, egg, and water. Drop the dough by the spoonful onto the prepared baking sheet, and press down on each cookie with a fork.

Bake for 20 minutes, or until golden and set. Let the cookies cool completely. Store in a tightly sealed container in the fridge, or freeze.

Bubble & Squeak Bites

MAKES 2–3 DOZEN TREATS

1 cup chopped roast beef, lamb, chicken, or turkey
1 cup chopped cooked vegetables, such as carrots, beans, or broccoli
½ cup mashed or boiled potatoes
1 large egg

Bubble and squeak is a traditional British dish made with the previous day's leftover roast and veg. It's generally cooked in a hot skillet until crisp (the steam creating the "squeak"), but here the ingredients are blended and baked to eat in one bite.

Preheat the oven to 350°F. Line 2 or 3 baking sheets with parchment paper.

In a large bowl or in the bowl of a food processor, combine the meat, vegetables, potatoes, and egg. If you want a finer texture, pulse the mixture in the food processor until as roughly or finely blended as you like.

Drop the mixture by the spoonful onto the prepared baking sheets, press down on each cookie with the back of a spoon, and bake for 20 to 25 minutes, or until set and springy to the touch. Let the cookies cool completely on the sheets. Store in a tightly sealed container in the fridge, or freeze.

**Ginger & Cinnamon Sweet
Potato Flax Squiggles**

Ginger & Cinnamon Sweet Potato Flax Squiggles

MAKES ABOUT 1½ DOZEN TREATS

1 cup mashed sweet potato

2 tsp grated fresh ginger

1 Tbsp canola oil or
   peanut butter

1 large egg

¾ cup ground flaxseed

½ tsp cinnamon

Mashed sweet potatoes are great for sweet treats. To make the mash, prick a whole sweet potato with a fork and stick it directly on the rack in the oven. Bake for 1 hour—you can do this while your oven is on for something else—then peel off the skin with your fingers and mash the soft flesh inside. The batter here is soft enough to squeeze out of a ziplock bag into shapes. You can, however, add more ground flaxseed or quinoa flour if you prefer to make a firmer dough that you can drop or roll and cut.

Preheat the oven to 350°F. Line a baking sheet with parchment paper.

In a medium bowl, mash the sweet potato with the ginger, oil, and egg using a potato masher or fork to get rid of all the lumps. Stir in the flaxseed and cinnamon.

Spoon the mixture into a heavy-duty ziplock bag, seal, and snip off one corner; squeeze the mixture out onto the prepared baking sheet, making letters, numbers, or shapes. (Alternatively, make long squiggles you can snip into small pieces once baked.)

Bake for 15 to 20 minutes, until deep golden. If you like, turn off the oven and leave the cookies inside to firm up as they cool. If you leave the cookies soft, store them in the fridge, or freeze. Otherwise they can be stored at room temperature in a tightly sealed container.

Chicken & Spinach Quinoa Cookies

1 cup chopped cooked chicken or turkey
1 cup fresh spinach
1 large egg
¾ cup quinoa flour or buckwheat flour

These crunchy chicken cookies make it easy for your pup to get his or her greens. Quinoa and buckwheat are technically seeds, but they can be found in flour form at most health food stores.

Preheat the oven to 350°F. Line a baking sheet with parchment paper.

In the bowl of a food processor, pulse the chicken, spinach, and egg, scraping down the sides of the bowl occasionally, until well blended. The mixture won't be perfectly smooth, but try to get rid of any big chunks.

Add the flour and pulse until the dough comes together in a ball. Roll the dough into 1-inch balls, place the balls on the prepared baking sheet, and flatten them with a fork. Alternatively, on a lightly floured surface, roll out the dough to ½-inch thick and cut into shapes or squares appropriate for the size of your dog.

Bake for 20 minutes, until pale golden around the edges and firm. If you like, turn off the oven and leave the cookies inside to harden as they cool. Store in a tightly sealed container in the fridge, or freeze.

Peanut Butter & Banana Treats

MAKES ABOUT 2 DOZEN COOKIES

1 ripe banana
¼ cup peanut butter
1 large egg
1½ cups chickpea flour

Chickpea flour is available—often in bulk—at most health food stores. It's made from ground dry chickpeas and provides all the nutrients and fiber of the whole legume. You could also make these treats with quinoa flour or buckwheat flour.

Preheat the oven to 350°F. Line 2 baking sheets with parchment paper.

In a medium bowl, mash the banana with the peanut butter and egg. Add the flour and stir or knead with your hands until you have a stiff dough.

On a lightly floured surface, roll out the dough to about ¼-inch thick. Cut into shapes with a cookie cutter or knife, and place the cookies on the prepared baking sheets.

Bake for 20 minutes, or until golden and firm. If you like, turn off the oven and leave the cookies inside to harden as they cool. Store in a tightly sealed container.

Ginger

Fishy Chickpea Treats

1 (6 oz) can tuna, salmon,
or sardines, drained
1 cup chickpea flour
1 large egg

Oily fish and ground chickpeas make for tasty, nutrient-dense treats that can be cut into any shape or size you like, whatever suits your pooch.

Preheat the oven to 350°F. Line a baking sheet with parchment paper.

In the bowl of a food processor, pulse the tuna, flour, and egg until it comes together and forms a ball. (If it's too wet and sticky, add more chickpea flour.)

On a lightly floured surface, roll out the dough to about ¼-inch thick and cut into whatever shapes you like.

Place the cookies on the prepared baking sheet and bake for 20 minutes, until golden and firm. If you like, turn off the oven and leave the cookies inside to harden as they cool. Store in a tightly sealed container in the fridge.

Beef & Buckwheat Bones

1 cup canned beef dog food
(not chunks in gravy)
1 cup buckwheat flour
1 large egg

Buckwheat is often categorized as a grain but is in fact a seed. Buckwheat contains more protein than grains and is rich in the amino acids that cereal crops lack. You can substitute chickpea flour, or for a grainy version, try whole-wheat, oat, or barley flour.

Preheat the oven to 350°F. Line a baking sheet with parchment paper.

In a medium bowl, stir together the dog food, flour, and egg until the mixture comes together, then turn the dough out onto a well-floured surface and knead until soft and smooth.

On a lightly floured surface, roll out the dough to about ¼-inch thick and cut into bones or other shapes with a cookie cutter. Place the bones on the prepared baking sheet and bake for 20 to 30 minutes, depending on their size, until firm. If you like, turn off the oven and leave the bones inside to harden as they cool. Store in a tightly sealed container in the fridge, or freeze.

Baby Food Bites

1 (2½ oz) jar beef or chicken stew baby food
1 cup chickpea flour

Jars of puréed baby food make great treats. Pick up some strained beef or chicken stew, or try puréed sweet potatoes—whatever your dog likes.

Preheat the oven to 350°F. Line 2 baking sheets with parchment paper.

In a medium bowl, stir together the baby food and flour until you have a stiff dough. (Add more flour if needed—chickpea flour can vary in texture.)

Roll the dough into small balls the size of marbles. Place the balls on the prepared baking sheets. Press down on each cookie with the tines of a fork, or with a bamboo skewer, making an X on each one.

Bake for 15 to 20 minutes, or until pale golden on the bottom and firm. If you like, turn off the oven and leave the cookies inside to harden as they cool. Store in a tightly sealed container.

TV Dinner Treats

1 cup sliced or shredded roast beef, pork, lamb, or chicken, chopped

1 cup boiled or roasted vegetables (carrots, broccoli, cauliflower, etc.), chopped

1 boiled potato, chopped

1 large egg

1 cup chickpea flour

Rather than wrap leftovers to reheat later, chop up the last of your roast, veg, and potatoes—all the elements of a TV dinner—and pulse them in a food processor with an egg and some chickpea flour. (For a grainy version of these treats, use whole-wheat, oat, barley, or brown rice flour—enough to make a soft dough.) The dough can be rolled, or cut into whatever shapes you like.

Preheat the oven to 350°F. Line 3 baking sheets with parchment paper.

In the bowl of a food processor, pulse the meat, vegetables, potato, and egg until well blended and pasty. Add the flour and pulse until the dough pulls away from the sides of the bowl and forms a ball.

Roll the dough into marble- or walnut-size balls and place them on the prepared baking sheets. Press down on each ball with the tines of a fork, or with a bamboo skewer, making an X on each one. Bake for 20 to 30 minutes, depending on their size, until pale golden and firm. If you like, turn off the oven and leave the cookies inside to harden as they cool. Store in a tightly sealed container in the fridge, or freeze.

Tuna Tater Tots

1 (6 oz) can tuna or salmon (packed in oil or water), undrained
1 cup instant mashed potato flakes

Made purely of tuna and potatoes, these flavorful bites are perfect for small dogs.

Preheat the oven to 350°F.

In the bowl of a food processor, pulse the tuna (with the liquid from the can) and potato flakes until well blended. Scrape down the sides of the bowl and let the mixture sit for a few minutes—this will allow the potato flakes to absorb some of the moisture from the tuna—then pulse again until well blended. The mixture should resemble fresh bread crumbs but hold together when squeezed. If the mixture is too dry to hold together, add a splash of water or stock.

Shape into marble-size balls or small cylinders and place on ungreased baking sheets.

Bake for 15 to 20 minutes, until firm. Cool on the baking sheets, and store in a tightly sealed container in the fridge, or freeze.

Cinnamon Banana Thumbprints

Thumbprints:

1 ripe banana

2 Tbsp canola or olive oil

1 to 1½ cups ground
  flaxseed

1 tsp cinnamon

Filling (optional):

¼ cup peanut butter

¼ cup cream cheese, at
  room temperature

Using ground flaxseed gives these cookies a nutty flavor and makes them high in fiber and rich in omega-3 fatty acids. (For a grainy version of these cookies, you can substitute oat or barley flour for the flaxseed.) To fancy them up, fill your thumbprints with a combination of peanut butter and cream cheese.

Preheat the oven to 350°F. Line 3 baking sheets with parchment paper.

In the bowl of a food processor, pulse the banana and oil until smooth. Add 1 cup of the flaxseed and the cinnamon and pulse until well blended; add more flaxseed as needed (it will depend on the size of the banana you use) until you have a soft dough.

Roll the dough into balls or drop with a small ice cream scoop onto the prepared baking sheets. Press down on each cookie with your thumb, making an indent. If using the filling, stir together the peanut butter and cream cheese and drop a small spoonful into each thumbprint. (Otherwise, leave them empty.)

Bake for 20 minutes, or until firm. Store in a tightly sealed container. If they are filled, store in the fridge, or freeze.

Cheesy Sweet Potato Treats

MAKES ABOUT 2 DOZEN COOKIES

1 cup grated old
  cheddar cheese
½ cup cooked and mashed
  sweet potato (see p. 110),
  squash, or carrots
1 large egg
¼ cup ground flaxseed
¼ cup quinoa flour or
  buckwheat flour

I haven't yet met a dog that doesn't love cheese. These treats can be made with mashed sweet potato, squash, or carrots. They cook up into light, crisp orange treats your pup will beg for.

Preheat the oven to 350°F. Line 2 baking sheets with parchment paper.

In a medium bowl or the bowl of a food processor, mash or pulse together the cheddar, sweet potato, and egg until well blended and any lumps of sweet potato have been worked out. Add the flaxseed and quinoa flour and stir until well combined.

Drop the dough by the spoonful onto the prepared baking sheets. Press down on each cookie with a fork (dip it in water to keep it from sticking). Bake for 20 minutes, or until pale golden and set. Let cool on the sheets, and store in a tightly sealed container in the fridge, or freeze.

Dogs have birthdays too, and if you're the type to celebrate, it's nice to bake a little something special, like pupcakes or brownies, for the party. Most of these recipes can be baked as squares, bars, or cupcakes. Softened spreadable cream cheese makes a simple "frosting," but don't be surprised if your dog licks it all off first. (They really are just like kids!)

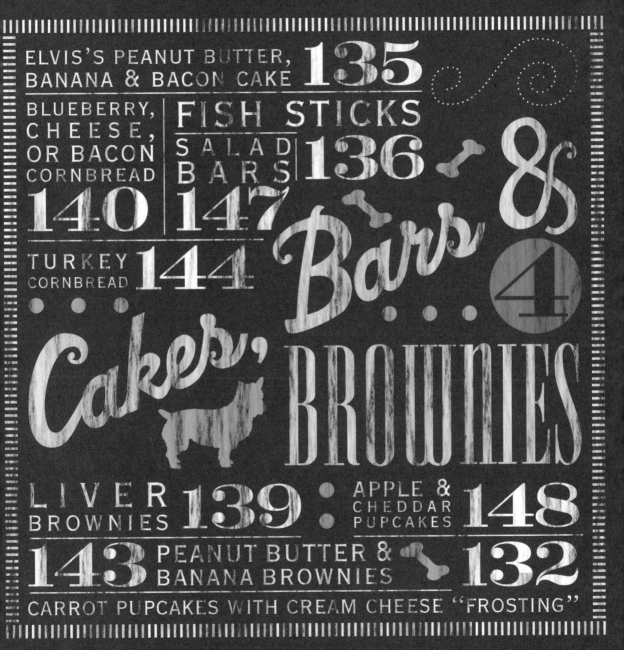

ELVIS'S PEANUT BUTTER, BANANA & BACON CAKE **135**

BLUEBERRY, CHEESE, OR BACON CORNBREAD **140**

FISH STICKS SALAD BARS **136**

147

8

TURKEY CORNBREAD **144**

Cakes, Bars & **4**

BROWNIES

LIVER BROWNIES **139**

APPLE & CHEDDAR PUPCAKES **148**

143 PEANUT BUTTER & BANANA BROWNIES **132**

CARROT PUPCAKES WITH CREAM CHEESE "FROSTING"

Carrot Pupcakes with Cream Cheese "Frosting"

MAKES 1 DOZEN REGULAR PUPCAKES, OR 2 DOZEN MINI

Cupcakes:

1 cup whole-wheat flour

1 tsp baking soda

¼ tsp cinnamon

½ cup applesauce

2 Tbsp canola oil

2 Tbsp honey

1 large egg

1 cup grated carrot
  (1 large carrot)

Frosting:

1 (8 oz) tub spreadable
  cream cheese, softened

1 Tbsp honey (optional)

If your pup's birthday celebrations call for cupcakes, this is the recipe. These cupcakes are even delicious enough to share with your dog. Party all around!

Preheat the oven to 350°F. Grease a regular muffin pan or 2 mini muffin pans.

In a large bowl, combine the flour, baking soda, and cinnamon. In a small bowl, stir together the applesauce, oil, honey, and egg. Add to the flour mixture, along with the carrot, and stir just until combined.

Divide the batter evenly in the prepared muffin pan and bake for 20 minutes, or until golden and springy to the touch. Transfer the pupcakes from the pan to a wire rack to cool.

To make the frosting, beat the cream cheese and honey (if using) until smooth, adding a little water as needed to achieve a spreadable consistency. Once the cakes are completely cooled, spread them with the frosting. Alternately, spoon the frosting into a ziplock bag, seal, snip off one corner, and squeeze out a swirl of frosting onto each pupcake. Store in a tightly sealed container in the fridge, or freeze.

Elvis's Peanut Butter, Banana & Bacon Cake

2 ripe bananas, mashed

¼ cup peanut butter

¼ cup canola oil

2 large eggs

2 Tbsp honey

1½ cups whole-wheat flour

¼ to ½ cup cooked and
crumbled bacon

1 (8 oz) tub spreadable
cream cheese, at room
temperature (optional)

The King made peanut butter, bananas, and bacon a popular sandwich; it turns out dogs love all three. The combo makes a pretty fantastic cake when it's time to celebrate a birthday or graduation from obedience school.

Preheat the oven to 350°F. Grease an 8- or 9-inch round or square cake pan.

In a large bowl, combine the bananas, peanut butter, oil, eggs, and honey, stirring until smooth (don't worry about getting all the lumps of banana out). Add the flour and bacon and stir just until combined.

Spread the batter into the prepared cake pan. Bake for 30 to 35 minutes, or until golden and springy to the touch. Cool for 5 minutes, then invert onto a wire rack to cool completely. If you like, frost with cream cheese, thinned with milk or water to achieve a spreadable consistency. Store in a sealed container in the fridge, or freeze.

**Hamish and
Jack the cat**

Fish Sticks

2 cups old-fashioned or
   quick-cooking oats
1 cup cornmeal
1 tsp dried parsley
   (optional)
1 (6 oz) can tuna, salmon,
   or sardines (packed in
   water), undrained
¼ cup water
2 Tbsp canola oil
1 large egg

This is one of my most requested recipes—every dog I know goes absolutely mad for these fish sticks. The omega-3 fatty acids found in tuna, salmon, and sardines can be good for skin conditions and arthritis in dogs.

Preheat the oven to 350°F. Coat a 13- x 9-inch pan with nonstick spray.

Place the oats in the bowl of a food processor and pulse until coarsely ground. Add the cornmeal and parsley (if using) and pulse to blend; transfer to a bowl and set aside. Place the tuna (with the liquid from the can) in the food processor with the water, oil, and egg, and pulse until well blended and almost smooth. Add to the oat mixture and stir until combined.

Press the mixture into the prepared pan, and cut into 24 strips (6 widthwise by 4 lengthwise) with a knife or pastry cutter.

Bake for 20 to 25 minutes, until golden and set. Let cool in the pan before separating into sticks. Store in a tightly sealed container in the fridge, or freeze.

Echo

Liver Brownies

1 lb beef liver

¼ cup canola oil

2 Tbsp honey

2 large eggs

1 cup whole-wheat
or barley flour

½ tsp baking powder

Of course a dog will appreciate a liver brownie far more than we would; they don't smell delicious in the oven, but your pup will appreciate the effort (and sacrifice).

Preheat the oven to 350°F. Coat an 8- x 8-inch pan with nonstick spray.

Cut the liver into chunks and place them in the bowl of a food processor. Add the oil, honey, and eggs, and pulse until well blended and as smooth as you can get it. Add a bit of water if the mixture seems too thick.

Scrape the batter into a bowl. Add the flour and baking powder and stir just until combined.

Spread the batter into the prepared pan. Bake for 25 to 30 minutes, until the top is springy to the touch. (If you have a small dog, you can bake the brownies in a 13- x 9-inch pan for 15 to 20 minutes—this will make thinner brownies that can be cut into smaller squares.) Let cool in the pan before cutting into squares. Store in a tightly sealed container in the fridge.

Blueberry, Cheese, or Bacon Cornbread

1½ cups cornmeal
1 tsp baking powder
1 tsp baking soda
1 cup buttermilk or
   thin plain yogurt
1 large egg
2 Tbsp canola oil
½ cup fresh or frozen
   blueberries, grated
   cheese, or cooked and
   crumbled bacon

This basic cornbread recipe can be dressed up with any number of ingredients—grated cheese, blueberries, crumbled bacon . . . It even makes a perfect vehicle for leftover bits of roasted meat or sausage. Anything goes!

Preheat the oven to 350°F. Grease an 8- x 8-inch pan with butter, or coat with nonstick spray.

In a medium bowl, combine the cornmeal, baking powder, and baking soda. In a small bowl, whisk together the buttermilk, egg, and oil. Add to the cornmeal mixture, along with the blueberries, cheese, or bacon, and stir just until blended.

Spread the batter into the prepared pan. Bake for 20 minutes, or until golden and firm. Let cool in the pan before cutting into small bars or squares. Store in a tightly sealed container in the fridge, or freeze.

Cola

Peanut Butter & Banana Brownies

1 cup mashed ripe bananas
(about 2 bananas)
½ cup peanut butter
2 Tbsp canola oil
2 Tbsp honey
2 large eggs
1 cup whole-wheat flour
1 tsp baking powder
¼ cup chopped peanuts
(optional)
½ (8 oz) tub spreadable
cream cheese, softened
(optional)

Overripe bananas are sweeter and more intensely flavored than those that haven't ripened yet. If you have some ripe bananas but aren't ready to bake, throw them in the freezer whole, in their skins; thaw on the countertop or in a bowl of hot water when you need them.

Preheat the oven to 350°F. Coat an 8- x 8-inch pan with nonstick spray.

In a large bowl, combine the bananas, peanut butter, oil, honey, and eggs. Add the flour, baking powder, and peanuts (if using), and stir just until blended.

Spread the batter into the prepared pan, and bake for 30 minutes, or until the top is springy to the touch. (If you have a small dog, you can bake the brownies in a 13- x 9-inch pan for 15 to 20 minutes—this will make thinner brownies that can be cut into smaller squares.) Let cool in the pan. If you like, frost the cooled brownies with cream cheese. Cut into squares. Store in a tightly sealed container in the fridge, or freeze.

Turkey Cornbread

1 cup whole-wheat flour
1 cup cornmeal
1 cup chicken or
    turkey stock
½ cup chopped leftover
    cooked turkey
    or chicken
¼ cup canola or olive oil
1 large egg

Humans aren't the only ones who appreciate leftovers from a big turkey dinner—those last bits of meat you pull off the bone after a big feast are ideal for adding to homemade dog treats. (If you use the carcass to make stock, you can use that here too.)

Preheat the oven to 350°F. Coat an 8- x 8-inch pan with nonstick spray.

In a large bowl, stir together the flour and cornmeal. In a medium bowl (or in the bowl of a food processor), stir or pulse together the stock, turkey, oil, and egg. Add to the dry ingredients and stir just until blended.

Spread the batter into the prepared pan, and bake for 25 to 30 minutes, until golden around the edges and springy to the touch.

Let cool, then turn out onto a cutting board and cut into squares appropriate for the size of your dog. If you want to make the treats crunchier, set the squares on a baking sheet, spacing them an inch or so apart, and return them to the oven for about 30 minutes. (They'll wind up more crunchy than hard.) Store in the fridge for up to 1 week, or freeze.

Salad Bars

MAKES 1–2 DOZEN BARS

Bars:

1 cup whole-wheat flour

1 tsp baking powder

½ tsp cinnamon

½ cup canned pure
pumpkin

½ cup peanut butter

2 large eggs

2 Tbsp tomato paste

2 Tbsp canola oil

1 Tbsp honey

1 large carrot, grated

½ (10 oz) package frozen
chopped spinach, thawed
and chopped again

Frosting (optional):

1 (8 oz) package cream
cheese, softened

1 Tbsp honey (optional)

When I was a kid, our family dog wouldn't touch a green vegetable. If we gave him beef stew, we would find all of the peas licked clean at the bottom of the bowl when he was done. These salad bars are a different story. They have pumpkin, carrot, tomato—even spinach—all whizzed into soft, cakey bars with a hint of peanut butter. For a celebratory cake, frost with whipped cream cheese.

Preheat the oven to 350°F. Coat an 8- x 8-inch pan with nonstick spray.

In a medium bowl, combine the flour, baking powder, and cinnamon. In a small bowl, stir together the pumpkin, peanut butter, eggs, tomato paste, oil, and honey. Add to the flour mixture, along with the carrot and spinach, and stir just until combined.

Spread the batter into the prepared pan, and bake for 25 to 30 minutes, until the top is springy to the touch. Let cool in the pan.

To make the frosting, beat the cream cheese and honey (if using) until smooth. Spread over the cake once it has completely cooled, then cut into squares or bars. Store in a tightly sealed container in the fridge, or freeze.

Apple & Cheddar Pupcakes

MAKES ABOUT 2 DOZEN PUPCAKES

1½ cups whole-wheat flour

¼ cup skim milk powder

1 tsp baking powder

Pinch cinnamon

1 cup cooked oatmeal, cooled

¾ cup water

1 large egg

2 Tbsp canola oil

1 large apple or ripe pear, coarsely grated (including the skin)

½ cup grated cheddar cheese

½ (8 oz) tub spreadable cream cheese, softened (optional)

Prepare a double batch of oatmeal the next time you make breakfast, and use the leftovers in these mini cakes. The batter can also be baked as a full-size cake in an 8- or 9-inch round or square cake pan.

Preheat the oven to 350°F. Coat 2 mini muffin pans with nonstick spray.

In a large bowl, combine the flour, skim milk powder, baking powder, and cinnamon. In a medium bowl, stir together the oatmeal, water, egg, and oil. Add to the dry ingredients, along with the apple and cheddar, and stir just until blended.

Fill the cups of the prepared muffin pans with the batter. Bake for 20 to 25 minutes, until the tops are springy to the touch. Let cool completely, and, if you like, spread the pupcakes with cream cheese. Store in a tightly sealed container, or freeze.

Maggie

These twice-baked Italian cookies—with their long shape and hard texture—are perfect for dogs. They keep well and have a crunch that dogs love. And of course a basic biscotti dough can be used as a blank canvas for meat, cheese, peanut butter ... anything your dog adores. To make smaller biscotti suitable for smaller dogs, divide the dough in half and shape it into two smaller, narrower logs before the first baking.

GINGER, APPLE & CINNAMON BISCOTTI

BEEF & CHEDDAR BISCOTTI **166**

169

PUMPKIN GINGERBREAD BISCOTTI **156**

5

OAT & HONEY BISCOTTI **152**

Biscotti

159

OAT & BANANA BISCOTTI

TURKEY DINNER BISCOTTI **155**

PEANUT BUTTER BISCOTTI

160

170

SPICED CARROT BISCOTTI

SALMON BISCOTTI **173**

BACON BISCOTTI **164**

Oat & Honey Biscotti

MAKES ABOUT 2 DOZEN BISCOTTI

3 cups whole-wheat flour

1 cup old-fashioned or
   quick-cooking oats

1 tsp baking powder

½ tsp cinnamon

1⅓ cups water

1 large egg

2 Tbsp canola oil

2 Tbsp honey

This basic biscotti formula can be jazzed up in myriad ways. Add any ingredients your dog loves: grated cheese, a spoonful of peanut butter, crumbled leftover meat—anything goes. They're also perfectly delicious plain.

Preheat the oven to 350°F. Line a baking sheet with parchment paper.

In a large bowl, combine the flour, oats, baking powder, and cinnamon. In a small bowl, stir together the water, egg, oil, and honey. Add to the dry ingredients and stir until the dough comes together.

Shape the dough into a log that's about 12 inches long, place it on the prepared baking sheet, and flatten it until it is 4 to 6 inches wide. If you like, brush the top with a little beaten egg to give it a shiny finish.

Bake for about 30 minutes, until firm. Reduce the oven temperature to 250°F. Allow the log to cool, and then cut it on a slight diagonal into ½-inch-thick slices, using a sharp, serrated knife. Place the biscotti upright on the baking sheet, keeping them spaced about ½ inch apart, and put them back in the oven for 1 hour. Store in a tightly sealed container.

Peanut Butter Biscotti

3 cups whole-wheat flour

½ cup wheat germ
   or oat bran

1 tsp baking powder

1 cup water

1 large egg

2 Tbsp skim milk powder
   (optional)

2 Tbsp canola oil

2 Tbsp honey

¾ cup peanut butter

½ cup chopped peanuts
   (optional)

**Inukshuk (left) and
Nikki (right)**

In addition to protein and fiber, peanuts and peanut butter also contain biotin, which is important for the metabolism of nutrients and the maintenance of skin, fur, and nails. And they're tasty too.

Preheat the oven to 350°F. Line a baking sheet with parchment paper.

In a large bowl, combine the flour, wheat germ, and baking powder. In a medium bowl, stir together the water, egg, skim milk powder (if using), oil, and honey. Add to the flour mixture, along with the peanut butter and peanuts (if using), and stir until the dough comes together.

Shape the dough into a log that's about 12 inches long, place it on the prepared baking sheet, and flatten it until it is 4 to 6 inches wide. If you like, brush the top with a little beaten egg to give it a shiny finish.

Bake for about 30 minutes, until firm. Reduce the oven temperature to 250°F. Allow the log to cool, and then cut it on a slight diagonal into ½-inch-thick slices using a sharp, serrated knife. Place the biscotti upright on the baking sheet, keeping them spaced about ½ inch apart, and put them back in the oven for 1 hour. Store in a tightly sealed container.

Pumpkin Gingerbread Biscotti

MAKES ABOUT 2 DOZEN BISCOTTI

3 cups whole-wheat flour
1 tsp cinnamon
1 tsp powdered ginger
½ tsp baking powder
1 cup canned pure pumpkin
¼ cup honey or molasses
2 Tbsp canola oil
1 large egg

Canned pumpkin makes for tasty biscotti that is rich in beta-carotene, and the cinnamon helps make your house smell fabulous—like pumpkin pie—as the cookies bake (unlike some of the other cookies in this book).

Preheat the oven to 350°F. Line a baking sheet with parchment paper.

In a large bowl, combine the flour, cinnamon, ginger, and baking powder. In a small bowl, stir together the pumpkin, honey, oil, and egg. Add to the flour mixture and stir until well blended.

Shape the dough into a log that's about 12 inches long, place it on the prepared baking sheet, and flatten it until it is 4 to 6 inches wide. If you like, brush the top with a little beaten egg to give it a shiny finish.

Bake for about 30 minutes, until firm. Reduce the oven temperature to 250°F. Allow the log to cool, and then cut it on a slight diagonal into ½-inch-thick slices using a sharp, serrated knife. Place the biscotti upright on the baking sheet, keeping them spaced about ½ inch apart, and put them back in the oven for 1 hour. Store in a tightly sealed container.

Oat & Banana Biscotti

MAKES ABOUT 2 DOZEN BISCOTTI

3 cups whole-wheat flour
1 cup old-fashioned or
    quick-cooking oats
1 tsp baking powder
½ tsp cinnamon
1⅓ cups water or
    chicken stock
1 ripe banana, mashed
1 large egg
2 Tbsp canola oil
1 Tbsp honey

To pretty these up for gifting, melt some carob chips to drizzle over the cooled biscotti, or dip the pieces of biscotti in the melted chips.

Preheat the oven to 350°F. Line a baking sheet with parchment paper.

In a large bowl, combine the flour, oats, baking powder, and cinnamon. In a small bowl, whisk together the water, banana, egg, oil, and honey. Add to the flour mixture and stir until well blended.

Shape the dough into a log that's about 12 inches long, place it on the prepared baking sheet, and flatten it until it is 4 to 6 inches wide. If you like, brush the top with a little beaten egg to give it a shiny finish.

Bake for about 30 minutes, until firm. Reduce the oven temperature to 250°F. Allow the log to cool, and then cut it on a slight diagonal into ½-inch-thick slices using a sharp, serrated knife. Place the biscotti upright on the baking sheet, keeping them spaced about ½ inch apart, and put them back in the oven for 1 hour. Store in a tightly sealed container.

Spiced Carrot Biscotti

MAKES ABOUT 2 DOZEN BISCOTTI

4 to 5 large carrots, scrubbed and cut into chunks
1 cup old-fashioned or quick-cooking oats
2 large eggs
2 cups whole-wheat flour
1/4 cup wheat germ
1/2 tsp baking powder
1/2 tsp cinnamon

Pieces of raw carrot are popular treats for some dogs I know. These cookies are made with cooked, mashed carrots rather than grated carrots, which makes them a great way to use up leftover veggies from dinner (or a good reason to make extra).

Bring an inch of water to a simmer in a medium saucepan. Add the carrots, cover, and cook until very soft. Drain, reserving the liquid, and mash the carrots. You should have about 2 cups of mashed carrots. In a small bowl, pour about 1 cup of the reserved cooking liquid over the oats and set them aside for about 10 minutes.

Preheat the oven to 350°F. Line a baking sheet with parchment paper.

Put the mashed carrots into a large bowl. Once they have cooled to lukewarm, stir in the eggs. Add the flour, wheat germ, baking powder, cinnamon, and oats, and stir until well blended.

Shape the dough into a log that's about 12 inches long, place it on the prepared baking sheet, and flatten it until it is 4 to 6 inches wide. If you like, brush the top with a little beaten egg to give it a shiny finish.

Bake for about 30 minutes, until firm. Reduce the oven temperature to 250°F. Allow the log to cool, and then cut it on a slight diagonal into ½-inch-thick slices using a sharp, serrated knife. Place the biscotti upright on the baking sheet, keeping them spaced about ½ inch apart, and put them back in the oven for 1 hour. Store in a tightly sealed container.

Bacon Biscotti

Bacon Biscotti

6 slices bacon

Canola oil, if needed

3 cups whole-wheat flour

1 cup old-fashioned or
   quick-cooking oats

1 tsp baking powder

½ cup water or
   chicken stock

2 large eggs

If you really want to score some points with your dog, save those bacon drippings you would most likely throw away and use them to make these hard and crunchy biscotti. If you're after small bacon-scented training treats, roll this dough into balls appropriate for the size of your dog, flatten them with your hand or the bottom of a glass (dogs aren't concerned with aesthetics), and bake them until firm.

Preheat the oven to 350°F. Line a baking sheet with parchment paper.

In a skillet set over medium-high heat, cook the bacon until crisp. Remove the bacon from the pan with a slotted spoon and set aside. Pour the drippings into a measuring cup; if you need to, add canola oil until you have ¼ cup.

In a large bowl, combine the flour, oats, and baking powder. In a small bowl, stir together the water, eggs, and bacon drippings. Add to the dry ingredients. Crumble the bacon and add it too. Stir until blended.

Shape the dough into a log that's about 12 inches long, place it on the prepared baking sheet, and flatten it until it is 4 to 6 inches wide. If you like, brush the top with a little beaten egg to give it a shiny finish.

Bake for about 30 minutes, until firm. Reduce the oven temperature to 250°F. Allow the log to cool, and then cut it on a slight diagonal into ½-inch-thick slices using a sharp, serrated knife. Place the biscotti upright on the baking sheet, keeping them spaced about ½ inch apart, and put them back in the oven for 1 hour. Store in a tightly sealed container in the fridge, or freeze.

Beef & Cheddar Biscotti

MAKES ABOUT 2 DOZEN BISCOTTI

3 cups whole-wheat flour

1 cup old-fashioned or
quick-cooking oats

1 tsp baking powder

½ cup grated cheddar
cheese

1⅓ cups beef or chicken
stock, or water

1 large egg

2 Tbsp canola oil or
beef drippings

½ to 1 cup cooked and
crumbled ground beef

Next time you cook up some ground beef, make extra to use in a batch of beefy biscotti for your pup. Finely chopped leftover roast beef, ground turkey or chicken, and chopped-up sausage meat all work well too.

Preheat the oven to 350°F. Line a baking sheet with parchment paper.

In a large bowl, combine the flour, oats, and baking powder; add the cheddar and toss to combine. In a small bowl, stir together the stock, egg, and oil. Add to the dry ingredients along with the beef, and stir until the dough comes together.

Shape the dough into a log that's about 12 inches long, place it on the prepared baking sheet, and flatten it until it is 4 to 6 inches wide. If you like, brush the top with a little beaten egg to give it a shiny finish.

Bake for about 30 minutes, until firm. Reduce the oven temperature to 250°F. Allow the log to cool, and then cut it on a slight diagonal into ½-inch-thick slices using a sharp, serrated knife. Place the biscotti upright on the baking sheet, keeping them spaced about ½ inch apart, and put them back in the oven for 1 hour. Store in a tightly sealed container in the fridge, or freeze.

Ginger, Apple & Cinnamon Biscotti

MAKES ABOUT 2 DOZEN BISCOTTI

3 cups whole-wheat flour
1 cup old-fashioned or
    quick-cooking oats
1 tsp baking powder
1 tsp cinnamon
½ tsp powdered ginger
1⅓ cups water or
    chicken stock
1 large egg
2 Tbsp canola oil
1 small apple, coarsely
    grated (including peel)

These tasty biscotti smell like apple pie as they bake.

Preheat the oven to 350°F. Line a baking sheet with parchment paper.

In a large bowl, combine the flour, oats, baking powder, cinnamon, and ginger. In a small bowl, whisk together the water, egg, and oil. Add to the flour mixture, along with the grated apple, and stir until well blended.

Shape the dough into a log that's about 12 inches long, place it on the prepared baking sheet, and flatten it until it is 4 to 6 inches wide. If you like, brush the top with a little beaten egg to give it a shiny finish, or sprinkle with more cinnamon.

Bake for about 30 minutes, until firm. Reduce the oven temperature to 250°F. Allow the log to cool, and then cut it on a slight diagonal into ½-inch-thick slices using a sharp, serrated knife. Place the biscotti upright on the baking sheet, keeping them spaced about ½ inch apart, and put them back in the oven for 1 hour. Store in a tightly sealed container.

Brisco

Turkey Dinner Biscotti

MAKES ABOUT 2 DOZEN BISCOTTI

3 cups whole-wheat
   or barley flour
1 cup old-fashioned or
   quick-cooking oats
1 tsp baking powder
½ tsp sage
1⅓ cups chicken or turkey
   stock, or water
2 large eggs
¼ cup turkey drippings
   or canola oil
½ to 1 cup chopped leftover
   roast turkey or chicken

A big holiday feast always provides leftovers that are perfect for dog treats. If you like, stir some leftover peas or mashed carrots into the dough as well.

Preheat the oven to 350°F. Line a baking sheet with parchment paper.

In a large bowl, combine the flour, oats, baking powder, and sage. In a small bowl, stir together the stock, eggs, and drippings. Add to the dry ingredients, along with the turkey, and stir until blended.

Shape the dough into a log that's about 12 inches long, place it on the prepared baking sheet, and flatten it until it is 4 to 6 inches wide. If you like, brush the top with a little beaten egg to give it a shiny finish.

Bake for about 30 minutes, until firm. Reduce the oven temperature to 250°F. Allow the log to cool, and then cut it on a slight diagonal into ½-inch-thick slices using a sharp, serrated knife. Place the biscotti upright on the baking sheet, keeping them spaced about ½ inch apart, and put them back in the oven for 1 hour. Store in a tightly sealed container in the fridge, or freeze.

Salmon Biscotti

MAKES ABOUT 2 DOZEN BISCOTTI

3 cups whole-wheat flour

1 cup old-fashioned oats

1 tsp baking powder

1 cup water

1 (7½ oz) can salmon (packed in oil or water), undrained

1 large egg

2 Tbsp canola oil

Dogs love it when there's something fishy going on—in the oven. Fatty salmon makes for heart-healthy, flavorful treats. Who would have thought you'd ever put it in a batch of biscotti?

Preheat the oven to 350°F. Line a baking sheet with parchment paper.

In a large bowl, combine the flour, oats, and baking powder. In the bowl of a food processor, pulse the water, salmon (with the liquid from the can), egg, and oil until smooth. Add to the dry ingredients and stir until the dough comes together.

Shape the dough into a log that's about 12 inches long, place it on the prepared baking sheet, and flatten it until it is 4 to 6 inches wide. If you like, brush the top with a little beaten egg to give it a shiny finish.

Bake for about 30 minutes, until firm. Reduce the oven temperature to 250°F. Allow the log to cool, and then cut it on a slight diagonal into ½-inch-thick slices using a sharp, serrated knife. Place the biscotti upright on the baking sheet, keeping them spaced about ½ inch apart, and put them back in the oven for 1 hour. Store in a tightly sealed container in the fridge, or freeze.

Kevin (left) and
Taylor (right)

Metric Conversions

Volume

¼ tsp	1 mL
½ tsp	2 mL
1 tsp	5 mL
2 tsp	10 mL
1 Tbsp	15 mL
2 Tbsp	30 mL
3 Tbsp	45 mL
4 Tbsp	60 mL
¼ cup	60 mL
⅓ cup	80 mL
½ cup	125 mL
⅔ cup	160 mL
¾ cup	185 mL
1 cup	250 mL
1⅓ cups	325 mL
1½ cups	375 mL
2 cups	500 mL
2½ cups	625 mL
3 cups	750 mL

Weight

½ lb = 8 oz	225 g
1 lb	454 g

Oven Temperatures

200°F	95°C
250°F	120°C
300°F	150°C
325°F	160°C
350°F	180°C
375°F	190°C
400°F	200°C

Cans, Jars, etc.

2½ oz	71 g
3¾ oz	106 g
6 oz	170 g
7½ oz	213 g
8 oz	226 g
10 oz	283 g
19 oz	540 g

Pans

8-inch	20 x 4 cm or 1.2 L
8 x 8-inch	20 x 20 cm or 2 L
9-inch	23 x 4 cm or 1.5 L
9 x 9-inch	23 x 23 cm or 2.5 L
13 x 9-inch	33 x 23 cm or 3.5 L

Length/Thickness

1/4 inch	6 mm
1/2 inch	1 cm
1 inch	2.5 cm
2 inches	5 cm
3 inches	8 cm
4 inches	10 cm
5 inches	12 cm
6 inches	15 cm
7 inches	18 cm
8 inches	20 cm
9 inches	23 cm
10 inches	25 cm
11 inches	28 cm
12 inches = 1 foot	30 cm
13 inches	33 cm
14 inches	35 cm

Index

Dog Photo Credits

Acknowledgments

In the Dog Kitchen would not have received the extreme makeover it did if not for the encouragement and creative mind of Taryn Boyd at TouchWood Editions—huge thanks for your support and vision. A big thank you to Pete Kohut for making the book look so pretty, and to Cailey Cavallin for her keen editor's eye. Thanks to my husband, Mike, for the behind-the-scenes research, photo culling, props painting, and kitchen cleaning. And the biggest hug to Lou, who is happier than anyone to see me every day.